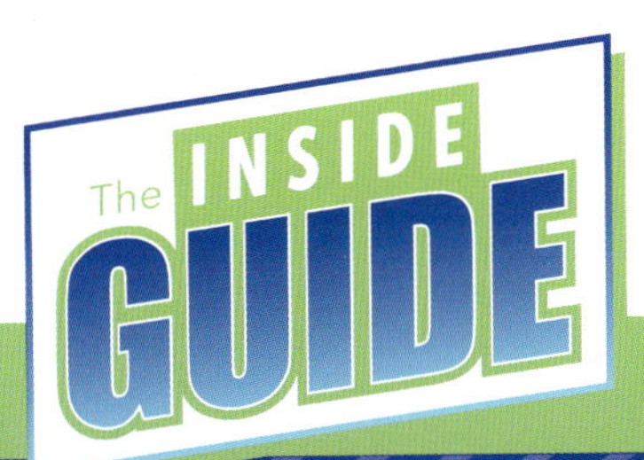

U.S. GOVERNMENT LEADERS

Choosing Supreme Court Justices

By Peter Finn

Published in 2025 by Cavendish Square Publishing, LLC
2544 Clinton Street Buffalo, NY 14224

Website: cavendishsq.com

Disclaimer: Portions of this work were originally authored by Barbara M. Linde and published as *Becoming a Supreme Court Justice*. All new material this edition authored by Peter Finn.

All websites were available and accurate when this book was sent to press.

Library of Congress Cataloging-in-Publication Data

Names: Finn, Peter, 1978- author.
Title: Choosing Supreme Court Justices / Peter Finn.
Description: Buffalo : Cavendish Square Publishing, 2025. | Series: The inside guide: u.s. government leaders | Includes index. | The highest court – Nominated, now what? – Joining the Justices – The work begins.
Identifiers: LCCN 2023054709 (print) | LCCN 2023054710 (ebook) | ISBN 9781502671493 (library binding) | ISBN 9781502671486 (paperback) | ISBN 9781502671509 (ebook)
Subjects: LCSH: United States. Supreme Court–Officials and employees–Selection and appointment–Juvenile literaure. | Judges–Selection and appointment–United States–Juvenile literaure.
Classification: LCC KF8776 .F56 2025 (print) | LCC KF8776 (ebook) | DDC 347.73/2634–dc23/eng/20231201
LC record available at https://lccn.loc.gov/2023054709
LC ebook record available at https://lccn.loc.gov/2023054710

Editor: Therese Shea
Copyeditor: Michele Suchomel-Casey
Designer: Deanna Lepovich

The photographs in this book are used by permission and through the courtesy of: Cover Joe Ravi/Shutterstock.com; p. 4 Poet Sage Photos/Shutterstock.com; p. 6 (top) Kate Way/Shutterstock.com; p. 6 (inset) John Jay (Gilbert Stuart portrait)/Wikimedia Commons; p. 8 VectorMine/Shutterstock.com; p. 9 Everett Collection/Shutterstock.com; p. 10 Ketanji Brown Jackson (robe photo)/Wikimedia Commons; p. 12 K2 images/Shutterstock.com; p. 13 DCStockPhotography/Shutterstock.com; p. 14 Courtesy of the Library of Congress; p. 15 (left) Attorney General Merrick Garland/Wikimedia Commons; p. 15 (right) Associate Justice Neil GorsuchOfficial Portrait/ Wikimedia Commons; p. 16 Supreme Court of the United States - Roberts Court 2022/Wikimedia Commons; p. 18 (left) The Swearing-in Ceremony of the Honorable Amy Coney Barrett (50546676973)/Wikimedia Commons; p. 18 (right) BarrettJudicialOath/ Wikimedia Commons; p. 19 Kagan Roberts and Obama/Wikimedia Commons; pp. 20, 22 Rob Crandall/Shutterstock.com; p. 21 Xinhua/Alamy Stock Photo; p. 24 stock_photo_world/Shutterstock.com; p. 25 Waxman during Hyatt III sketch/Wikimedia Commons; p. 26 (left) Ruth Bader Ginsburg 2016 portrait/Wikimedia Commons; p. 26 (right) Antonin Scalia Official SCOTUS Portrait/Wikimedia Commons; p. 27 lensfield/Shutterstock.com; p. 29 (left) Steven Frame/Shutterstock.com; p. 29 (right) artboySHF/Shutterstock.com.

Some of the images in this book illustrate individuals who are models. The depictions do not imply actual situations or events.

CPSIA compliance information: Batch #CSCSQ25: For further information contact Cavendish Square Publishing LLC at 1-877-980-4450.

Printed in the United States of America

CONTENTS

Supreme Court justices meet in the Supreme Court Building in Washington, D.C.

THE HIGHEST COURT

Disagreements come up in our daily lives. Sometimes people are able to come to a decision together about how to move forward. Other times, they need someone else to decide who is right and who is wrong. When these disagreements have to do with the law, that "someone else" might be a judge in a court.

Courts are at nearly every level of government in the United States and include state, town, and city courts. Courts decide how the law applies in different situations. Judges help interpret the law for citizens when the law isn't clear. If one of the parties in a case doesn't agree with a court's decision, they can ask a higher court to hear the case. The highest court in the United States is the Supreme Court.

Fast Fact

All U.S. states have state supreme courts. The U.S. Supreme Court is a federal court.

Justices of the Judicial Branch

The judges of the Supreme Court usually rule on cases that have to do with the U.S. Constitution and other federal, or national, laws. They explain what these laws mean and how they apply to a case. The court can also **overturn** laws that don't agree with the

Americans sometimes gather outside the Supreme Court Building when a case that affects their lives is being heard.

Constitution. These duties have a real impact on people's lives.

The judges that serve on the U.S. Supreme Court are called justices rather than judges to show that they're different from judges of the lower courts, or the other courts in the country. A Supreme

In 1789, President George Washington appointed the first Supreme Court chief jusice, John Jay, shown here, and five associate justices.

CHECKS AND BALANCES

The U.S. government is made up of three branches. The legislative branch, including the House of Representatives and the Senate, makes the laws. The executive branch, headed by the president, executes, or carries out, the laws. The judicial branch decides if the laws are legal according to the U.S. Constitution. The Supreme Court and lower federal courts make up the judicial branch. Each branch has powers that the others don't. Each branch also has ways of checking another branch's power. For example, the president can **veto** potential laws, and the Supreme Court can overturn laws if they're unconstitutional. This arrangement among the branches of government is called checks and balances.

Court justice is a member of the **judicial** branch of the U.S. government.

Congress first set the number of Supreme Court justices at six in the Judiciary Act of 1789, the law that established the federal court system. This number was changed to nine justices in 1869.

Fast Fact

You might see the name of the Supreme Court of the United States shortened to "SCOTUS" in the news. This term was first used in 1879.

Qualifications

The Constitution established the Supreme Court and how the justices would be chosen. They aren't elected as with many other federal

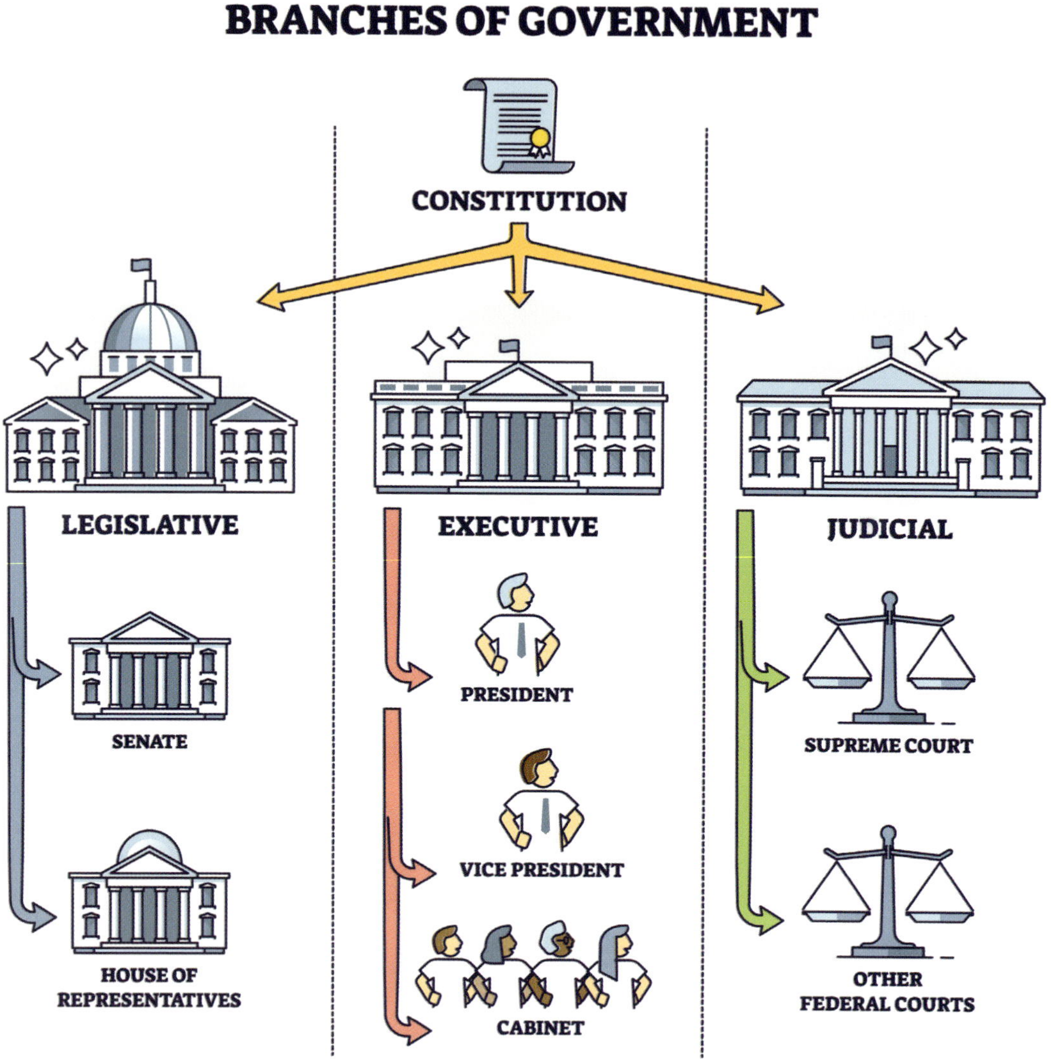

BRANCHES OF GOVERNMENT

CONSTITUTION

LEGISLATIVE

SENATE

HOUSE OF REPRESENTATIVES

EXECUTIVE

PRESIDENT

VICE PRESIDENT

CABINET

JUDICIAL

SUPREME COURT

OTHER FEDERAL COURTS

The Supreme Court has the power of judicial review, which means it can decide if acts of Congress or state legislatures are unconstitutional.

jobs. Instead, the president selects them, commonly from a list made beforehand of suitable candidates. The president often chooses someone in the same **political party** as them and who has similar ideas about how the country and government should be run. The president then

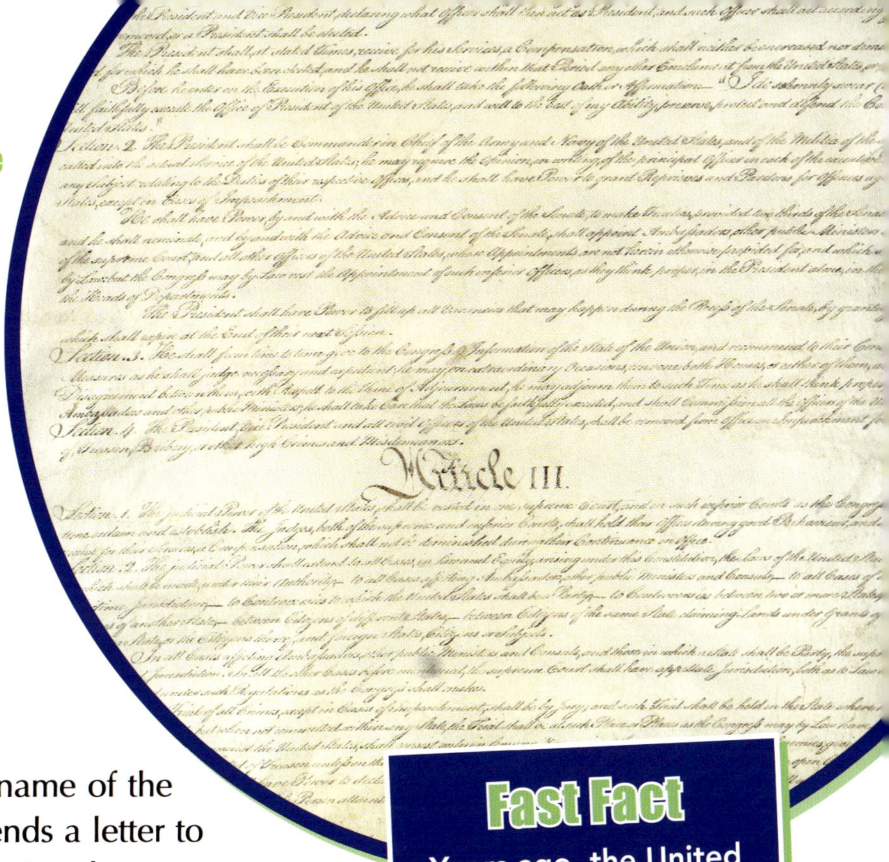

Article III of the U.S. Constitution established the Supreme Court, calling it "one supreme Court."

announces the name of the **nominee** and sends a letter to the Senate informing them.

The Constitution doesn't say what a justice's qualifications—their skills, experience, and knowledge—should be. However, all Supreme Court justices to date have been lawyers, also called attorneys, or have at least studied law. Many justices have even argued cases before the Supreme Court as lawyers. Some have been judges in lower courts. All must have a good record of public service. Their professional lives must be outstanding, and they should be upstanding citizens in their personal lives too.

Fast Fact

Years ago, the United States had few law schools. Instead, law students learned from working with practicing lawyers.

In 2022, Ketanji Brown Jackson became the first Black woman to serve as a Supreme Court justice.

NOMINATED, NOW WHAT?

Openings don't come often on the nine-person Supreme Court. Why? A justice can hold that position for the rest of their life. They can also choose to retire at any point, though.

When an opening does occur, the president selects someone to be a justice. However, that isn't the end of the process. It's a nomination, which means it's a proposal that someone will be a good fit for the office. After that, the Senate—the upper house of the U.S. Congress—must confirm, or approve, the candidate.

The Judiciary Committee

A group in the Senate called the Judiciary Committee may take about a month to collect information about the nominee. The senators on the committee want to find out as much as they can about the nominee's past jobs and actions to determine how they might handle the job of a justice.

> **Fast Fact**
> The U.S. Senate Committee on the Judiciary, also known as the Senate Judiciary Committee, oversees the Department of Justice (DOJ).

The Senate holds hearings in which they ask the nominee challenging questions. These hearings can be long

In this photo, future justice Sonia Sotomayor speaks to the Senate Judiciary Committee about her nomination.

and tiring for the nominee. They usually last four or five days but can take longer than that, depending on the nominee. The hearings are public so all American citizens can watch the proceedings.

After the hearings are finished, the Judiciary Committee votes on the nomination. It sends a recommendation to the full Senate that the nominee be confirmed or rejected—or the committee may send no recommendation at all.

Next, the entire Senate **debates** about the nominee and then votes. For decades, the nominee needed what was called a supermajority, or 60 senators voting yes, to be confirmed. However, in 2017, that

The Senate Judiciary Committee is a standing committee, which means it's permanent. It includes 21 senators.

number was lowered to 51. If a tie occurs, the vice president, who **presides** over the Senate, makes the deciding vote. If the nominee isn't approved, the president starts over with another nominee.

Fast Fact

A 60-vote supermajority is still needed for legislation to pass through the Senate.

Politics

Most Americans agree that Supreme Court justices should be above politics, or the power struggle between political parties in government. They say justices should not make decisions in cases according to their personal political views but should be **impartial** and decide according to the Constitution. This way, all citizens are treated fairly. However, keeping personal political ideas out of decisions isn't easy, and justices commonly have connections to a political party.

THE FIRST WOMAN JUSTICE

In 1981, President Ronald Reagan's nominee, Sandra Day O'Connor, became the first woman on the Supreme Court. Becoming a Supreme Court justice can sometimes take months, but O'Connor was nominated on August 19, 1981, and confirmed for the position on September 21, 1981. O'Connor had overcome discrimination. No law firm would hire her as an attorney after she graduated law school in 1952. However, she excelled in her government work. Her confirmation as a Supreme Court justice encouraged many women to go to law school and enter politics. O'Connor retired from the Supreme Court in 2006 and died in 2023.

In 2009, Sandra Day O'Connor was awarded the Presidential Medal of Freedom, the highest civilian honor in the United States.

Merrick Garland was nominated to be a justice by Democratic president Barack Obama in 2016. The Republican-led Senate decided not to act on the nomination. When Republican Donald Trump became president in 2017, he nominated Neil Gorsuch, who was confirmed.

Fast Fact

When the president and the majority of the Senate belong to the same party, it's much more likely that the nominee will be confirmed.

In fact, just as presidents typically choose Supreme Court candidates that have views that align, or agree, with their own, senators vote for or against candidates for that same reason. A nominee's record of what they say publicly or how they ruled in court cases if they were a lower-court judge has an impact on whether they'll be confirmed by the Senate.

As of 2023, 17 chief justices and 104 associate justices have served on the Supreme Court.

JOINING THE JUSTICES

After a justice has been confirmed by the Senate, they have a swearing-in ceremony, in which they take two oaths of office. These are promises to the American people, and they're required under Article IV of the U.S. Constitution. Traditionally, the chief justice of the Supreme Court administers, or gives, the oaths to the new justice, although other court officers may do it.

Taking the Oaths

In the Constitutional Oath, the justice says: "I, ________, do solemnly swear (or affirm) that I will support and defend the Constitution of the United States against all enemies, foreign and domestic; that I will bear true faith and allegiance to the same; that I take this obligation freely, without any mental reservation or purpose of evasion; and that I will well and faithfully discharge the duties of the office on which I am about to enter. So help me God."

Fast Fact

William Howard Taft served as president of the United States before he became the chief justice of the Supreme Court. He said it was a greater honor than being president.

In these photographs, Justice Amy Coney Barrett takes the two oaths of office in October 2020.

In the Judicial Oath, the justice promises: "I, ________, do solemnly swear (or affirm) that I will administer justice without respect to persons, and do equal right to the poor and to the rich, and that I will faithfully and impartially discharge and perform all the duties incumbent upon me as ________ under the Constitution and laws of the United States. So help me God."

Sometimes a justice chooses to say a combination of these two oaths. The ceremony may be public or private. Family and friends often attend. The president might be there too.

The Chief

A Supreme Court justice is either one of the eight associate justices or the chief justice. It's not necessary that the chief justice already be an associate justice. Some candidates are nominated to be chief justice. The

SUPREME COURT TRADITIONS

Before taking the oaths, the new justice sits in the chair that belonged to Chief Justice John Marshall, who served from 1801 to 1835. While being sworn in, justices may put their hand on a Bible. They may also choose to put their hand on a copy of the Constitution, a different religious writing, or nothing at all. Often, the justice's spouse holds the text, but someone else special to the person may as well. After taking the oaths, the new justice and the chief justice walk down the steps of the Supreme Court Building, both wearing their black robe. The black robe tradition began around 1800.

Justice Elena Kagan smiles with President Barack Obama and Chief Justice John Roberts before her swearing-in ceremony, also known as an investiture.

After Chief Justice William Rehnquist died in 2005, President George W. Bush nominated John Roberts to become not just a justice but the new chief justice.

Fast Fact

The actual title of the chief justice of the Supreme Court is Chief Justice of the United States.

chief justice presides over the court. They act as a kind of supervisor or manager as the court does its work. Some of these actions include overseeing the selection of cases appropriate for the Supreme Court to hear, the dates when these cases will be heard or decided, the rules about the case discussions

In addition to many other duties, the chief justice presides over presidential impeachment trials. There have been four such trials as of 2023.

Fast Fact

The chief justice acts as the representative for the United States in judicial matters with other countries.

among the justices, and the votes about the cases.

If the chief justice is in the majority for a case opinion, meaning they have the same opinion as more than half the justices deciding a case, the chief justice chooses whether to write the majority's opinion or have another justice write it. The chief justice also oversees the work of the more than 500 other people who work in and around the Supreme Court, including librarians, police officers, and others.

The phrase "Equal Justice Under Law" is written above the western entrance of the Supreme Court Building.

THE WORK BEGINS

Each year, the Supreme Court gets more than 7,000 **petitions** to hear cases, but it hears oral arguments for only about 80 cases. Hearing oral arguments means the court listens to opinions and facts from the lawyers on both sides of a case and asks them questions before making a decision. The court also makes decisions on cases without hearing oral arguments.

The Supreme Court considers only cases that may challenge a federal law or part of the Constitution. Most often, these cases are **appeals** from lower courts. Four justices must vote "yes" for the case to come before the Supreme Court.

Fast Fact

The request for the Supreme Court to review a case is called a petition for writ of certiorari. A writ of certiorari is an order from a superior court to a lower court for the record of a case.

A Day in Court

The Supreme Court's term begins on the first Monday in October and runs through the next October. However, the justices have a summer recess beginning in late June or early July.

Usually, oral arguments are heard on Mondays, Tuesdays, and Wednesdays.

This is the inside of the Supreme Court Building.

The justices line up in order of seniority and walk into the courtroom that way. The chief justice sits in the middle. The next two most-senior justices sit next to the chief justice on either side.

Two cases are often heard in a day, with each side of a case being given 30 minutes to present their argument.

Fast Fact

Attorneys arguing in front of the Supreme Court address Chief Justice John Roberts as "Mr. Chief Justice" and the associate justices as "Justice [last name]" or "Your Honor." A female chief justice will likely be addressed as "Madam Chief Justice" as they are in lower courts.

The public can usually sit in on these hearings too. The justices listen carefully and ask questions.

Fast Fact

The Supreme Court makes audiotapes of oral arguments and opinions available to the public.

Justices' Conferences

After the oral arguments are heard, justices' conferences are held. Before these private meetings, the Supreme Court justices shake hands to show they're partners under the law. They speak about the case in order of seniority, starting with the chief justice and then the associate justice

The Supreme Court of the United States doesn't allow cameras in the courtroom when the court is in session. However, people can draw sketches like this, which shows an attorney arguing in front of Justices Elena Kagan and Brett Kavanaugh.

INTERPRETATIONS OF THE CONSTITUTION

Using the Constitution to decide cases may sound simple, but it isn't—even after the justices discuss the arguments with each other. Some justices try to interpret the Constitution according to what they think its authors meant when it was written. They think the Constitution's meaning is fixed, or unchanging. This theory is called originalism. Another theory is called living constitutionalism. Those who believe in this idea think the Constitution's meaning changes with the times and with the values and beliefs of the American people. Justices may make decisions according to one of these theories.

Justices Ruth Bader Ginsburg and Antonin Scalia were famously close friends who had opposite views of the Constitution. Ginsburg said, "The Constitution we revere and enforce is not ... frozen in 1787." Scalia said, "The Constitution that I interpret and apply is not living but dead, or as I prefer to call it, enduring."

This is the Great Hall, which leads into the SCOTUS courtroom.

who has served longest and so on.

Finally, the justices go in the same order to voice their decision in the case. If the decision is split, one of the justices is assigned the job of writing the opinion of the court for the majority. A justice who dissented from this opinion, or didn't agree with it, is assigned to write the dissenting opinion. Still, the majority's opinion is the last word on the case. No other court or lawmaker in the whole country can change a Supreme Court decision.

Supreme Court justices decide what government agencies can and can't do. They decide what is and isn't included in people's constitutional rights. They change lives. It's critical that the best candidates are selected and confirmed—for the good of the nation.

FAMOUS CASES AND DECISIONS OF THE SUPREME COURT

***Marbury v. Madison* (1803)**
SCOTUS can review and rule on laws and presidential actions.

***Brown v. Board of Education* (1954)**
Separate schools for different races are not equal.

***Gideon v. Wainwright* (1963)**
People who cannot afford a lawyer must be provided with one.

***Miranda v. Arizona* (1966)**
Police must tell suspects their rights before questioning them.

***Loving v. Virginia* (1967)**
People have the right to marry others of different races.

***Tinker v. Des Moines* (1969)**
Students have constitutional rights in school.

***Roe v. Wade* (1973)**
State legislation restricting the ending of pregnancies is unconstitutional.

***Obergefell v. Hodges* (2015)**
Same-sex marriage is legal and constitutional.

***Dobbs v. Jackson Women's Health Organization* (2022)**
The Constitution doesn't protect the right to end a pregnancy, overturning *Roe v. Wade*.

THINK ABOUT IT!

1. Do you think the Supreme Court should have more or fewer justices, or should the number remain nine? Why?
2. Do you think it's possible to separate politics from the Supreme Court? Why or why not?
3. Do you think the public should be able to hear the justices' discussions in their private conferences? Why or why not?
4. Which theory of constitutional interpretation do you favor, and why?

GLOSSARY

appeal: A legal process by which a case decided in a lower court is brought to a higher court to review the decision.

debate: To formally and publicly discuss or argue.

impartial: Fair; treating all people the same.

impeachment: The process of charging a public official with misconduct.

judicial: Having to do with justice and the courts.

nominee: Someone nominated, or suggested, for a position or honor.

overturn: To change a court decision or ruling.

petition: An official written request to have a case decided by a court of law.

political party: A group whose members hold the same general beliefs about how government should work and who work to fill government positions with people in their party.

preside: To lead or to be in a position of authority.

veto: To reject a proposed law.

FIND OUT MORE

Books

Abramson, Jill. *What Is the Supreme Court?* New York, NY: Penguin Workshop, 2022.

Magoon, Kekla. *Ketanji: Justice Jackson's Journey to the U.S. Supreme Court*. New York, NY: Quill Tree Books, 2023.

Tolli, Jenna. *Inside the Supreme Court*. New York, NY: Rosen Publishing, 2021.

Websites

Judicial Branch—The Supreme Court
www.ducksters.com/history/us_judicial_branch.php
Check out more information about this part of the U.S. government and your legal rights.

Landmark United States Supreme Court Cases
www.americanbar.org/groups/public_education/programs/constitution_day/landmark-cases/
Discover the importance of the court's work through these cases.

Supreme Court of the United States
www.supremecourt.gov
Learn much more about SCOTUS's history and work here. You can even listen to live audio.

Publisher's note to educators and parents: Our editors have carefully reviewed these websites to ensure that they are suitable for students. Many websites change frequently, however, and we cannot guarantee that a site's future contents will continue to meet our high standards of quality and educational value. Be advised that students should be closely supervised whenever they access the internet.

INDEX